Weather

Richard Worsnop

Contents

Introduction   3
Weather forecasting   4
Looking at clouds   8
Rain   10
Snow   11
Storms   12
Hail   14
Fog   15
Weather around the world   16
Freak weather   22
Glossary   24
Index   24

7323

Introduction

The weather is important to all of us. When the weather is bad, it can be difficult for people like fishermen, sailors, farmers and pilots to do their jobs. You may want to know if the day will be hot or cold, or wet or dry.

Weather forecasting

Each day, the weather **forecast** is read on the television and radio.

In newspapers, maps give weather forecasts. **Symbols** are used on weather maps to show different kinds of weather.

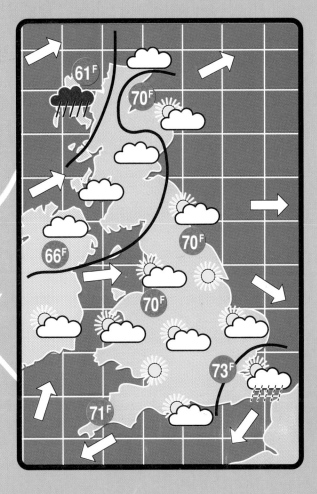

Here are some symbols which are often used in weather forecasts.

cloudy

rain

sunny

snow

storms

sunny spells

direction of wind

sunny spells and showers

People who study the weather are called meteorologists. They have weather balloons, computers and satellites to help them. ▼

Satellites take photographs ▶ of the earth from space. This is the kind of picture satellites send back to help meteorologists. You can see the outline of Europe. The white part shows the thick clouds. The darker part is the sea. The little bits of white are small patches of cloud.

Looking at clouds

Clouds are made from millions of water **droplets** or tiny pieces of ice. There are many different kinds of clouds. Not all clouds bring rain.

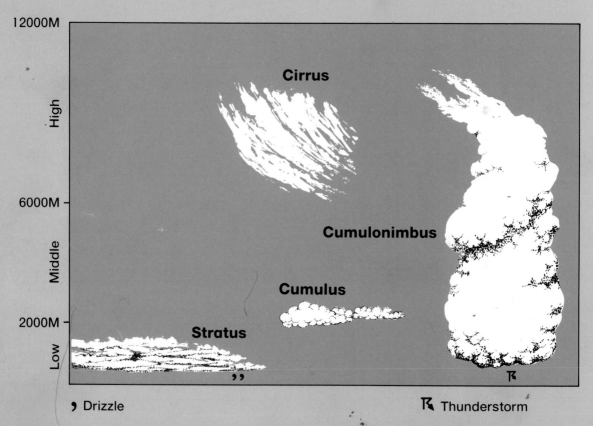

This drawing shows you four different kinds of cloud. Some are higher in the sky than others.

Cirrus clouds are very high
up in the sky and are made
from tiny pieces of ice.
You can see them when
the weather is fine.

Cumulus clouds are made
from water droplets.
They look like cotton
wool. You can usually
see these clouds in fine
weather. If cumulus
clouds get big, the
weather can get **stormy**.

Stratus is a layer of cloud
which is low in the sky.
Clouds like this give very
fine, light rain called drizzle.

Rain

The millions of water droplets in clouds sometimes bump into each other and make bigger drops. The bigger drops are too heavy to float in the air. These drops fall as rain.

Snow

Snow is **feathery** bits of ice, made in clouds where the air is freezing.

This is what a snowflake looks like close-up

Storms

This is a cumulonimbus cloud, or thundercloud.
Clouds like this bring stormy showers of rain, snow or hail.
Cumulonimbus clouds also bring thunder and lightning.

Thunder and lightning happen at the same time. Lightning travels much faster than thunder, so we see it before we hear the thunder.

Hail

Cumulonimbus clouds also bring hail. These clouds are very tall. When the air inside the cloud is very strong, it blows the water droplets up and down. The droplets freeze at the top and bottom of the cloud. They fall to the ground as small lumps of ice, called hailstones.

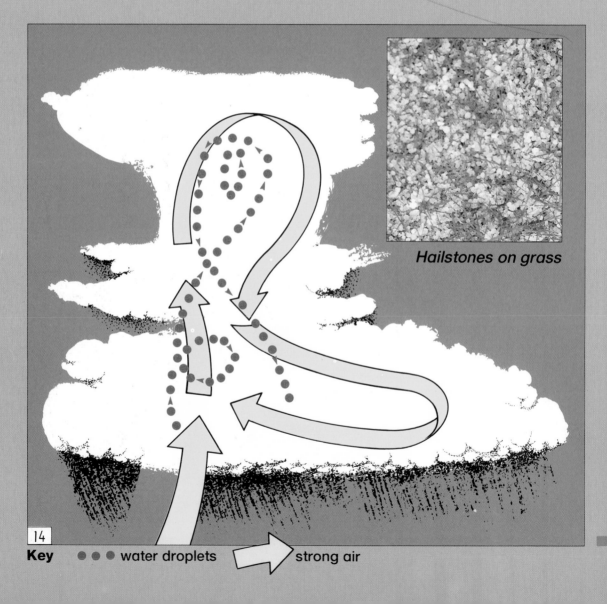

Hailstones on grass

Key ●●● water droplets ⇒ strong air

Fog

Fog is a thin cloud which is so low that it touches the ground. The air feels wet when it is foggy.

Weather around the world

In Britain, the weather is always changing. It does not usually stay hot or cold, or wet or dry for very long. The weather can change so quickly that, sometimes, the sun comes out when it is still raining. When this happens, the sun shines through the raindrops and makes a rainbow.

In some parts of the world, the weather does not change very much.

In some hot countries, it hardly ever rains. In this **desert**, in Namibia, Africa, it might rain only once in four or five years.

In other countries, it often rains very heavily. Heavy rainfall can cause **floods**. Floods can cause damage and make everyday life very hard for people.

India

This man is in the Antarctic, where it is always very cold. He has thrown some water into the air. The air is so cold that the water has frozen immediately.

In very hot countries, people often see heat hazes. When the sun is very hot it heats the air. The air rises and mixes with dust. This makes a heat haze.

Chile, South America

Freak weather

Very unusual weather is called freak weather.

In 1984, a freak hailstorm in Germany damaged this car. Giant hailstones like these can be the size of golf balls. They can damage **crops** and houses.

This hailstone fell in Cardiff, in 1968. It was 8½ cm wide.

A freak wind has turned this plane over.

Shoreham Airport, England

Glossary

crops   Crops are plants which are grown for food.

desert   A desert is a very dry place with little water.

droplets   A droplet is a tiny drop.

feathery   If something is feathery it is divided into lots of thin parts so that it looks soft.

floods   A flood is a rush of water caused by heavy rainfall.

forecast   To forecast the weather means to say what you expect the weather to be like.

stormy   If the weather is stormy, there are strong winds and heavy rain, hail, thunder and lightning.

symbol   A symbol is a picture used to represent something.

Index

cloud 7-12, 14-15
desert 18
drizzle 9
floods 19
fog 15
forecast 4
freak weather 22-23

hail 12, 14, 22
heat haze 21
lightning 12-13
meteorologists 6
rain 10, 12
rainbow 16-17
satellite 6-7

snow 11, 12
symbols 5
storms 9, 12-13
thunder 12-13
wind 23